"I DIDN'T BELIEVE
THE EARLY-AMERICAN ARTS
AND CRAFTS
HAD BEEN GIVEN
THE RECOGNITION
THEY DESERVED
SO I ASSEMBLED
EXAMPLES OF ARCHITECTURE,
FURNITURE,
AND WIDELY DIVERGENT
EARLY-AMERICAN MATERIALS
OF ALL SORTS
TO SHOW AMERICA
AS IT HAD BEEN."

Henry Francis du Pont

Discover the
Winterthur Period Rooms

by Pauline K. Eversmann

Table of Contents

1

*A*lmost forty years after he first inherited his family home at Winterthur, Henry Francis du Pont explained his motivation in creating more than 175 period rooms. He said it was a desire to "show America as it had been" that led him to build a large addition to his home, especially designed to accommodate historic architectural interiors. These interiors then became the backdrop for the display of du Pont's growing collection of antique furniture, silver, needlework, textiles, paintings, prints, ceramics, and glass.

Henry Francis du Pont was born in 1880 at a time when an increasing number of Americans began to worry that their material heritage was not being properly preserved. However, rather than display the arts and crafts of early America in a traditional manner—namely, in cases and on platforms in art museum fashion—they sought instead to recreate early American interiors through the use of period rooms. The period room as a display technique gained popularity in America during the second half of the nineteenth century. As early as 1850, Benjamin Pereley Poore of West Newbury, Massachusetts, used architectural elements from historic American structures such as Boston's John Hancock house to create period rooms in his home, Indian Hill. A decade later in Brooklyn, New York, a sanitary fair introduced the general public to the concept of period rooms by featuring a New England

Henry Francis du Pont
Du Pont (1880–1969) became the fifth owner of Winterthur in December 1926, and he continued to develop and enhance the estate throughout his lifetime.

Left: Winterthur Museum.

kitchen as one of its displays. The 1876 Centennial Exposition in Philadelphia showcased a New England log house as a centerpiece exhibit. By the early twentieth century, the Essex Institute of Salem, Massachusetts, opened three alcoves displaying a New England kitchen as well as an 1800 bedroom and parlor. These alcoves, open on one side to allow the public easy viewing, were furnished with an eye to historical accuracy. The rooms conveyed the illusion of daily occupancy through carefully placed accessories of everyday life, such as spectacles, a newspaper, and a work basket filled with knitting needles and half-finished work.

All of these displays proved extremely popular with viewers, who found the sight of objects arranged in architectural settings much more compelling than static displays of the same objects in museum cases. A period room conveyed a sense of activity, as though the occupants had just stepped outside for a moment and would return shortly. This was history infinitely more interesting than what could be found in the pages of a textbook or behind glass in a museum, and Americans, already influenced by the patriotic fervor surrounding the Centennial, enthusiastically embraced period room installations and historic houses such as Mount Vernon.

What was lost in the public's love affair with period rooms was the understanding that these displays, whether in historic houses or museums, did not and could not accurately convey life "as it had been." In the

first place, the period rooms were frozen in time: all of the objects represented a single style period, as though the owners purchased a complete household of new furnishings and tossed everything else out. Lost was the sense of accumulation over time. In a real eighteenth-century household, seventeenth-century chests surely continued to live in the same room with new rococo high chests, and yet period rooms seldom displayed the two together. Lost also was the inevitable clutter, the dust, and certainly the smells and noises of real life. Even such carefully researched installations as the Brooklyn Museum's nineteen period rooms, which opened in 1919, or the landmark 1924 American Wing of the Metropolitan Museum of Art represented a presentist view of the past—the past as seen from a twentieth-century perspective.

McIntire Bedroom

The furnishings and upholstery in this room are all in the federal style, exemplifying a common approach to period room decorating. The room illustrates a "textbook" approach to a style period rather than an actual historical setting.

4

Pennsylvania German Fraktur

Frequently created as baptismal records, family documents, or memorials, these elaborate certificates often feature birds, hearts, and religious symbols.

At the same time that museums turned to the period room display technique, prominent American collectors and decorators also began to use historic architecture to create period rooms in their own homes, most notably Isabella Stuart Gardener at Fenway Court in Boston and Henry Davis Sleeper at Beauport in Gloucester, Massachusetts. Historical accuracy was not a primary goal for America's early preservationists and collectors. Rather, their concerns centered on evoking the spirit of early America, both in its crafts and its craftsmen.

This, then, was the environment in which Henry Francis du Pont came of age and which he enthusiastically embraced. All of these early installations influenced du Pont's decision to use the period room technique, first in his summer home in Southampton, Long Island, and then at Winterthur, the 2,400-acre estate that he inherited on the death of his father in 1926. At Winterthur, this meant that elaborately carved seventeenth-century chests and elegant silver tankards from Massachusetts found a compatible home in a New England interior from the same date; delicate plaster decoration from Baltimore was paired with equally delicate inlaid furniture from the same city; and the interiors of a Pennsylvania farmhouse provided an appropriate backdrop for the ironwork and decorated documents, or Fraktur, of the Pennsylvania Germans.

Like much else that du Pont tackled throughout his long life, the period room project was marked by his exceptional vision and attention to detail and was executed on a lavish scale. Once he had decided to display his growing collection of American decorative arts in period rooms, he began a massive expansion of the Winterthur house that essentially tripled it in size. The addition took the form of a long, narrow extension that ran from north to south and cut into the steep hillside behind the back of the house. This design allowed for the installation of rooms on either side of central hallways, thus providing natural light via windows in all of the rooms. Due to the steepness of the hillside, the addition stood eight stories high at the south end.

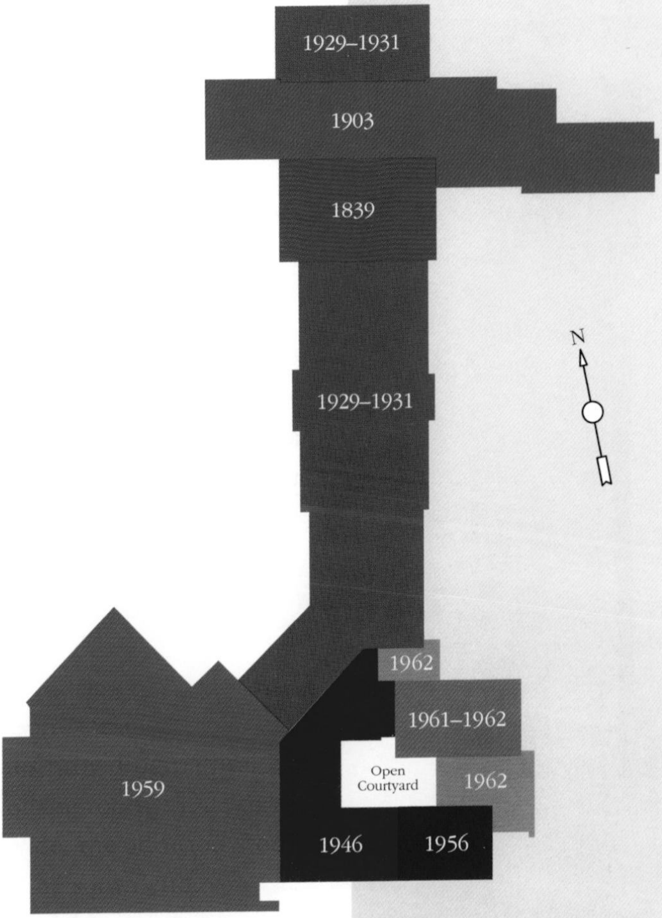

1929–1931

1903

1839

1929–1931

N

1962

1961–1962

Open Courtyard

1962

1959

1946

1956

Museum Expansion

This plan of Winterthur Museum shows the many stages of the building's construction.

6

*W*ith the first period rooms at Winterthur, which were installed between 1927 and 1932, du Pont sought to create a home in the tradition of an English manor house. In these rooms he would not only display his growing collection of American decorative arts but also entertain family and friends in a grand manner. Thus, many of the original period rooms bore names such as "Reception Room," "Ladies' Room," "Smoking Room," and, as testimony to his lavish lifestyle, "Visiting Maid's Pressing Closet." To create these spaces, du Pont purchased interior architecture from houses such as Belle Isle in Virginia, Port Royal in Philadelphia, and Readbourne in Maryland. Although du Pont wrote to a colleague that he was "doing the house archaeologically correct," correspondence with his chief architect, Albert Ely Ives, indicates that his interpretation of archaeological correctness differs from our perception today.

One of the best examples of the way in which du Pont used architecture is his installation of the Port Royal Entrance Hall and Port Royal Parlor. Architecture for these two spaces came from a country home constructed in 1762 on Frankfort Creek, outside Philadelphia. Built as a summer home by Edward Stiles, a wealthy merchant, the house was named for Port Royal, Bermuda—Stiles's birthplace. The architecture exemplifies eighteenth-century design; its classical features,

Left: Port Royal Entrance Hall.

Port Royal Parlor

Eighteenth-century homeowners valued balance, harmony, and order—qualities that have been re-created here in the symmetrical arrangement of the furniture, in the careful attention to color, and in the proportion of the furnishings to room size.

such as the entablature, or molding, around the room and Palladian windows, represented for du Pont the highest achievement of American craftsmen. However, when the architecture was brought to Winterthur, du Pont was more concerned with creating spaces suitable for entertaining and for the proper display of his collection than with the historical accuracy of the installations. For example, he instructed Ives to lengthen the main entrance hall to accommodate another staircase installation (Readbourne Stair Hall) that was to run parallel to the Port Royal Entrance Hall. In addition, du Pont altered the original woodwork finish, which had been painted to resemble wood paneling; instead, du Pont painted the woodwork a soft green and installed eighteenth-century Chinese wallpaper in the area over the wainscoting.

The effect is stunning even today, enhanced by the artful placement of matching Chippendale marble-top tables, a ten-foot tall-case clock, and two large gilt mirrors that reflect the glow of brass sconces and candlesticks. For all its grandeur, however, the room is not a historically accurate re-creation. In fact, were Edward Stiles to return to life, it is doubtful that he would recognize his old entrance hall.

In the adjoining Port Royal Parlor, du Pont asked that the area between the windows be widened to accommodate two Philadelphia high chests that he hoped to obtain and position on either side of the room. Today, Port Royal Parlor appears remarkably similar to du Pont's first installation of the room. In many ways, it embodies the essence of du Pont's early approach to period room design and decoration. The central focus of the room is an outstanding collection of elaborately carved Chippendale-style furniture crafted in Philadelphia between 1755 and 1780. The ornateness of the furniture, however, is tempered by its placement within the classical framework of the Port Royal Parlor architecture.

Arranged with careful attention to symmetry and balance, Port Royal Parlor can be divided into mirroring halves. Du Pont succeeded in obtaining the two beautiful Philadelphia high chests that he specifically wanted for the room, and they now face each other from the east and west walls of the room. Flanking the fireplace (centrally located on the south wall) are a rare pair of matching Chippendale sofas that are highly valued for having been owned by patriot John Dickinson. Balancing the high chests and sofas in perfect placement are tea tables, side chairs, and easy chairs. A tall desk-and-bookcase stands opposite the fireplace on the north wall, and the entire arrangement is

What is the Chippendale style?

As practiced in America, the Chippendale style was based on the design books of English cabinetmaker Thomas Chippendale. In Philadelphia cabinetmakers bowed to their clients' preference for deeply carved, highly curved interpretations of the style and produced some of the most elaborate furniture made in the colonies. Features included intricately pierced chair backs, cabinet fronts aswirl with carvings of leaves and shells, and heavily ornamented pediments on the tops of high chests and desks.

10

Du Pont Dining Room

Formal dinners in early America focused on presentation and display. Servants followed elaborate diagrams in arranging dishes, glassware, and silver. A host was judged at least as much on how his table was set as on how his food tasted.

anchored by a large oriental carpet with a golden ground that echoes the golds of the upholstery.

This parlor was originally called the "Reception Room," and it was there that du Pont entertained his numerous weekend guests. He also received his large extended family there on New Year's Day, when they practiced the French custom of paying short, ceremonial calls on relatives and close friends. In both Port Royal Parlor and Port Royal Entrance Hall, du Pont sought to evoke the spirit of an age—the age of enlightenment—rather than capture the precise nature of an eighteenth-century interior. Like many of his contemporaries, du Pont glorified the age of enlightenment, which he felt represented the best of the American past. The superb craftsmanship of Philadelphia furnituremakers symbolized the colonists' wisdom, dedication, and pursuit of excellence. These virtues stood in stark contrast to early twentieth-century perceptions about the inferiority of machine-made products from the industrial revolution. By using these rooms to receive and entertain visitors, du Pont expressed his views more eloquently than any political tract or newspaper editorial ever could.

An equally romantic view of the past can be seen in the Du Pont Dining Room, situated directly above Port Royal Parlor. It too features expanded eighteenth-century woodwork, in this case from Readbourne, a home built in the 1740s in Centreville, Maryland. By furnishing the space in the popular federal style, du Pont paid tribute to the time after the American Revolution when the new nation turned its attention to establishing its own identity as a republic and adopted a federalist form of government. To convey the patriotic intent of this room, du Pont chose to display several icons of American history, including Benjamin West's unfinished painting, *Peace Commissioners,* which shows men preparing to sign the treaty that ended the Revolution (shown right); a portrait of George Washington by Gilbert Stuart; and the only known set of six tankards made by patriot and goldsmith Paul Revere (shown right).

From the time the room was finished in the late 1920s until 1950, when the du Ponts moved out in preparation for the reconfiguration of the house into a museum, the dining room served as the hub of activity. The du Ponts loved to host family celebrations and lavish weekend parties in this room. Here, visitors to Winterthur enjoyed meals prepared from food grown on the Winterthur estate, and they were served at a table set with imported ceramics especially

What is the federal style?

The federal style celebrates the rediscovery of ancient civilizations in the eighteenth century, using such classical symbols as eagles, wheat sheaves, and urns as carved and inlaid decoration on objects. Much of the furniture from this era loosely imitates the designs of ancient Greek and Roman furniture. With such obvious references to the classical past, it was a style perfectly suited to the new United States, which patterned its government in form and principle on the Roman republic.

Cecil Bedroom

The focal point of this room is the unusual, pad-foot, maple Queen Anne bed made in Rhode Island between 1735 and 1750.

The Cecil Bedroom fireback came from the Elk Ridge Furnace in Maryland.

selected by du Pont to match the floral arrangements in the room. Nineteenth-century American glassware and silver completed the elegant table settings.

Du Pont's desire to create a country home in the tradition of the grand English country houses was certainly realized in rooms such as the Port Royal Parlor and the Du Pont Dining Room, but large rooms for entertaining were not the only period rooms developed during this early period. Du Pont also used smaller architectural settings to create bedrooms, hallways, and more intimate parlors. He chose for his own bedroom—now called Cecil Bedroom—a space on the seventh floor of the wing that overlooked the garden. There he installed unique architecture from Cecil County, Maryland, that represents the attempt of a country craftsman to duplicate the classical style so favored in urban areas. Although the craftsman understood the visual vocabulary of classicism, including the use of columns, capitals, and entablatures, he lacked the understanding of proportion and relationships so necessary for the successful adaptation of classical architecture to eighteenth-century domestic spaces. The result, although it lacks the authenticity of the Port Royal rooms, nonetheless still conveys the interest in the classical past that dominated craft activity in the colonial era.

For this softly colored, fully paneled room, du Pont surrounded himself with objects in the elegant Queen Anne style, one of his favorite design periods. He juxtaposed the gently curved chairs and chests from New England with a japanned high chest. The result adds texture and contrast to an otherwise serene composition. The furniture co-exists peacefully with wonderful examples of needlework—both framed pictures and bed hangings—whose colors complement the faded tone of the woodwork. An added personal touch is a unique iron fireback in the fireplace with an inscription that reads, "At Elk Ridge Furneis as you See, William Williams, he Mad[e] me, In the Year of 1/Thousand/762." Elk Ridge Furnace was an ironworks located on the Patapsco River in Maryland.

In his careful selection of compatible objects for each newly created space, du Pont strove to give his rooms a lived-in look. He sought out quantities of small objects to place on tables or hang on the walls in order to give each room a human dimension and convey something of real life through casual groupings. It took a true artist, however, to achieve a homelike (rather than cluttered) appearance, and du Pont was indeed a true artist when it came to decorating. He had a

13

What is the Queen Anne style?

The beauty of the Queen Anne style depends largely on subtlety of line and curve rather than on carving or inlaid decoration. There were exceptions to this rule, of course, and the use of a highly ornate and colorful decorative technique called "japanning" is one of these (see below). In japanning, a piece of furniture is covered with layers of paint and plaster decoration to imitate lacquerwares associated with the Orient.

feel for color, proportion, and balance that served him well as he arranged and rearranged each space until it was just right.

Du Pont's ability to take disparate elements and weave them

Chinese Parlor

This room was created from two rooms in the original Winterthur house, and its size was determined by the wallpaper. Du Pont was particularly pleased with the effect created by the green damask curtains and upholstery.

into a whole is nowhere better illustrated than in the Chinese Parlor. In 1929 he took three spaces from the original 1839 house (the dining room, a stairway, and a hallway) and created one room to serve as a showcase for an eighteenth-century Chinese wallpaper that depicted scenes of everyday life in a Chinese village. The motifs of the wallpaper, including fretwork, upturned pagoda leaves, and straight-leg furniture, visually unite a room that would otherwise seem fragmented. The room has more than thirty pieces of furniture from different regions of colonial America, including Philadelphia, New York, Boston, and Newport, Rhode Island. The Chinese theme is continued with examples of Chinese lacquerwork and export porcelain. Joe Kindig, Jr., an antiques dealer from York, Pennsylvania, and a good friend of du Pont, once remarked, "Harry du Pont is like a conductor of music. He may not know how to play each and every instrument, but he knows how to blend them together, exquisitely." He may well have had the Chinese Parlor in mind when he made this statement.

Throughout the house, du Pont carefully orchestrated not only the interior spaces but also the exterior views. The views from every room were carefully planned to allow du Pont to remain constantly in touch with his beloved landscape, a landscape on which he lavished the same care, the same attention to detail, and the same concern for balance, proportion, and color that characterized his work within the house. From windows in his new wing, he could watch the seasons change—from the soft green of the newly leafed spring trees to the cooling green of full summer to a blaze of autumn color to the stark grays of winter with the surrounding trees silhouetted against the sky.

By the end of 1932, perhaps worn out by the intense activity of the previous five years, du Pont wrote to a good friend and fellow collector, "In fact the whole house is settled." And, to Thomas Waterman, a young architect and recent acquaintance of du Pont's, he sent a letter stating, "My house here is completely finished." Despite this declaration, du Pont was soon to begin the second great phase of period room installations at Winterthur, for it was in that same year that he turned his attention to the unaltered section of the house he had inherited from his father.

Thomas Waterman
Waterman served as du Pont's chief architect from 1933 until his death in 1951. The two developed a close personal relationship; over the years, Waterman became less a teacher and more a collaborator.

Bottom left: Detail of the wallpaper in the Chinese Parlor. Beautifully hand-painted in China, these scenes of Chinese life helped to satisfy Western curiosity with exotic locales and Far Eastern culture.

Refining the Period Rooms

*I*n retrospect it seems ironic that du Pont wrote to Waterman of his house's completion since he and Waterman would collaborate for the next eight years on the total reinstallation of his father's Victorian interiors, situated in the north end of the house. His association with Waterman, an architect involved in the Colonial Williamsburg restoration and head of the Historic American Buildings Survey, also marks a new phase in du Pont's approach to period room installations. Under Waterman's tutelage, his awareness of issues of historical accuracy increased, although he would still make many decisions based primarily on aesthetic considerations. While he continued to supplement historic architecture with modern millwork to fit existing spaces, he began to seek historical examples and documentation for doing so.

Du Pont's transformation of his father's imposing entryway—with its large marble staircase in the beaux arts style, which had been so popular at the turn of the century—exemplifies his new approach to the installation of historic architecture. He tore out the existing staircase and woodwork, replacing them with delicate neoclassical plaster ornamentation and woodwork. He had acquired these architectural features from an 1822 plantation home called Montmorenci built in Shocco Springs, North Carolina. The centerpiece of the room is a graceful,

Montmorenci Stair

Although du Pont had hoped to use the original staircase from Montmorenci in his installation, it turned out to be structurally unsound and not suited to the space and height requirements of the stair hall at Winterthur. Du Pont collaborated with Thomas Waterman in the redesign, extending the original one-story staircase to two stories and, most importantly, widening the circular shape to an elliptical oval that completes a 360-degree turn as it reaches for the ceiling.

Left: Montmorenci Stair Hall.

Chinese Export Porcelain Bowl

A continuous scene of horses, hunters, and hounds preparing for a fox hunt decorate this punch bowl. An inscription painted in the center of the bowl proclaims "SUCCESS TO THE SOUTHERN HUNT."

elliptical staircase that soars two stories. The design of the staircase was based on the original from Montmorenci, a circular stair only one story high. In changing the shape of the original staircase, du Pont worked closely with Waterman to find historical precedents for the design he wanted. In 1935 he sent a photograph to Waterman, explaining, "I am also enclosing a photograph of a staircase in an old house which has an elliptical well, so you will see that we are not breaking all precedents by making our well elliptical."

While the Montmorenci staircase remains the focus of the room today and is, to many, the most enduring image of Winterthur, there is much else to be admired in the space. In keeping with the date of the original architecture, du Pont furnished the room with accessories in the later federal style, including a matching suite of furniture made by a member of the Seymour cabinet-making family of Boston, a pier table from New York labeled by Charles-Honoré Lannuier, and a portrait of a young girl clad in classical dress. A large Chinese export porcelain punch bowl on top of the pier table serves as a reminder of the opening of trade with China in 1784. The room remains a tribute not only to du Pont's genius for creating harmonious settings but also to the new nation he sought to honor by displaying the fruits of its craftsmen. Objects from New England, the Mid-Atlantic region, and the South signify and celebrate the early republic.

Despite mutual agreement that any new installations were to possess a greater degree of "authenticity" than the earlier period rooms, du Pont and Waterman did not always share the same definition of what was "authentic." Many of the period rooms created during this second phase of installation reflect a compromise between their two views. In a small room on one of the bedroom floors, du Pont argued against Waterman's design for an entablature to complete a window installation because the original window did not have this particular architectural feature. Disappointed that du Pont had rejected his plan to improve on the original, Waterman wrote to him, "I am sorry you decided against the entablature for the window in Nemours . . . the trim without the entablature is illiterate." Du Pont relented and had an entablature made that would be "tried out." He left the final decision to one of his closest friends and advisers, Bertha Benkard. Mrs. Benkard decided in favor of the entablature, and it graces the Nemours Room to this day.

Mrs. Benkard played a similar role as decisionmaker in the subsequent 1938 installation of the Flock Room. Installed using

Mrs. Harry Horton Benkard

Distinguished collector of eighteenth- and nineteenth-century furniture, Mrs. Benkard was a good friend of Henry Francis du Pont's sister, Louise du Pont Crowninshield, and shared du Pont's passion for the decorative arts of early America. Together, they worked on Winterthur's period rooms, spending countless hours finding just the right fabric, the perfect object, the most appropriate design motif for each space. Following Mrs. Benkard's death in 1945, du Pont wrote to her daughter, Mrs. Bertha Rose, "Without your mother Winterthur would never have been what it is today."

19

Flock Room

The painting above the fireplace is original to the woodwork and is considered among the earliest American landscape paintings. Henry Francis du Pont wrote to a friend that the Flock Room "is going to be very handsome. . . . the big fireplace with the paintings above it and the flock wallpaper will be a wonderful setting for my William and Mary furniture."

architecture from Morattico Hall, a 1715 Virginia home, the Flock Room represented a new standard for accurate installations at Winterthur but, again, compromises were required. After considering several locations within the house for the architecture, du Pont and Waterman selected an area originally occupied by the billiard room. One of the prime considerations in this choice was that it allowed the room to be installed as close to its original dimensions as possible. Determining those dimensions required all the skill the architect possessed.

Morattico Hall had been dismantled more than ten years before du Pont purchased the woodwork. The architecture had been dispersed, some used to create a summer cottage on the Morattico property and some stored under the eaves of the cottage. Du Pont later purchased architectural elements from the cottage, and it was during the removal of the reused Morattico architecture that the other architectural elements were discovered. It then fell to Waterman to reconstruct the original rooms. First, he located an old photograph of the house; then, relying on clues provided by the architecture itself, he painstakingly put all the pieces of the puzzle together, producing four floor plans from which to choose. Each plan represented a varying degree of historical accuracy. After consultations with Mrs. Benkard, du Pont chose the second-most accurate plan. One of the more interesting aspects of the installation of the Flock Room is the incorporation of three painted panels that du Pont had purchased years earlier and had hung in the Wentworth Room. The panels were originally from Morattico Hall, and through the Flock Room installation, they were returned to their original architectural setting.

Named the Flock Room in recognition of a rare English wall covering of canvas with flocked velvet design, the room contains a special collection of turned chairs and tables in the William and Mary style. The overall appearance of the room bears the hallmark of a Waterman/du Pont collaboration. The architecture re-creates an important Virginia home, one that emulated the prevailing English taste: large scale, bold architectural details; a huge fireplace; and painted woodwork. The room exemplifies the quintessential du Pont furnishing plan: the subtle, harmonious color combinations; the careful arrangement of small objects to create a lived-in look; and the repetition of a dominant design motif, in this case the twisted turnings of the furniture, metalwork, and glassware.

What is the William and Mary style?

Strong vertical lines, attenuated proportions, and baroque carving mark the William and Mary style. In particular, the style favored the use of a twisted and spiral column—as seen on the table legs in the Flock Room (left).

The Cadwalader Connection

Many of the Blackwell Parlor objects were made for Gen. John Cadwalader of Philadelphia. A man of considerable wealth and position, Cadwalader served with distinction during the Revolution. His own town house may well have looked very much like Winterthur's Blackwell Parlor (shown above) both in furnishings and architectural details.

Another room installed at this time was also designed to complement an exceptional architectural interior. In 1937 du Pont purchased woodwork from the home of a Philadelphia matron, Mrs. Frank McFadden. The architecture originally had been part of an elaborate town house built in 1764 at 224 Pine Street in Philadelphia. Named the Stamper-Blackwell House after its first two owners, the house contained some of the most elaborate and intricately carved interior architecture ever produced in Philadelphia, a perfect backdrop for the elaborate and intricately carved Chippendale furniture made in Philadelphia at the same time. Du Pont, who had a distinct fondness for this style of furniture, was delighted to acquire the architecture and immediately set about designing the room that would be called Blackwell Parlor. In his correspondence with Waterman, it is interesting to note how he moved into a more active role as designer. At one point, he wrote to Waterman, "I am still struggling with the Blackwell house room . . . as soon as I can get the practical details worked out, I shall have Leslie [Potts, du Pont's estate manager] send you prints for you to put the finishing touches on." Whatever the struggles, the end result was worth it. Nestled in an intimate parlor setting are examples of the very finest carved furniture produced in Philadelphia in the third quarter of the eighteenth century: chairs, tea tables, gaming tables, looking glasses, and easy chairs echo the workmanship of the deeply carved mantel and architectural moldings.

In the years since du Pont first furnished the Blackwell Parlor, the room has continued to evolve as the collection has expanded. Today, three portraits by John Singleton Copley, fine English glass, and imported Chinese ceramics complement the simplicity of American needlework pictures and a prayer book cover displayed in the room. A visitor to the Blackwell Parlor gains a sense not only of the opulent lifestyle of wealthy eighteenth-century Philadelphians but also of the essential vision of Henry Francis du Pont, who wished to honor the fine craftsmanship and aesthetic vision of colonial Americans.

The Four Continents

These delicate Chinese export porcelain figurines represent the four continents or quarters of the globe: Africa, Europe, Asia, and America. Made in Derby, England, about 1748–1848, this rare set is on display in Blackwell Parlor.

23

he evidence suggests that during the second phase of period room installations, du Pont began to consider the possibility of turning Winterthur into a museum. In 1938 he wrote to William Sumner Appleton of the Society for the Preservation of New England Antiquities, saying of his home, "This may be a museum some day." His vision is evident in the creation of period rooms intended not only for entertaining or for everyday use but rather for show, for the display of du Pont's extraordinary collection of American decorative arts.

In a small space that had once housed the family's squash court, du Pont installed paneling from the 1670 Thomas Hart house of Ipswich, Massachusetts. He then furnished the room, now known as the Hart Room, with his choice collection of seventeenth-century furniture, silver, and ceramics. The vertical forms of the paneling follow the attenuated lines of turned chairs. The careful attention to detail in a chamfered (shaped) ceiling beam is also seen in the elaborate carving on the chests. The muted colors of the room are offset by the glow of seventeenth-century American silver, much of it used originally for religious purposes.

What is the seventeenth-century style?

Whether in architecture or furniture (such as the court cupboard in the Hart Room, above), the seventeenth-century style emphasizes verticality and relies on elaborate turnings, bold carvings, and painted decoration. These design elements were brought from England by the early colonists, who followed the traditions of their homelands in the New World.

Left: The Court.

Tappahannock Room

The architectural elements in this room are from the Ritchie house, built about 1690, in Virginia. The raised paneling is a unique configuration found in only one other Virginia home.

The World War II years represented a period of rest in the heretofore almost ceaseless work of installing and reinstalling period architecture at Winterthur. Like the rest of the world, the du Ponts turned their attention to conserving and preserving precious natural resources for the war effort. In 1946, however, following the peace treaties, activity resumed once again at Winterthur. There was now little doubt that du Pont envisioned his home as a potential museum. In a letter written many years later in response to a request for an interview, du Pont stated, "I realized that the collection was too good to be dispersed after my death and hence the idea of a museum gradually came to me." Still working in concert with Waterman, he began to plan for the removal of such country house amenities as the Dancing Room, Badminton

Court, and Bowling Alley. These spaces were all replaced with historic architecture. Attention to accuracy once again dominated this final planning phase. In the ongoing correspondence with Waterman concerning new installations, the word *authentic* appears repeatedly. When designing a room to fit into the space occupied by the former Dancing Room, Waterman wrote to du Pont, "Enclosed is a plan of the Tappahannock Room showing the proposed changes . . . It will make a very good room and I will be happy to say that it is authentic."

The Tappahannock Room's architecture comes from a 1725 home, the Ritchie house, built on the banks of the Tappahannock River in Virginia, although the paneling probably dates from 1740 or later. For its time, the architecture is remarkably complex and sophisticated. The paneling features three-part vertical panels with the top level forming a frieze of small squares. This arrangement, rare in Virginia houses of the period, seems to indicate that the craftsman who created it was acquainted with English design sources and may even have read Joseph Moxon's 1703 book, *Mechanick Exercises,* or at least knew of its principles. Moxon describes a process for wainscoting that is very similar to the Tappahannock paneling.

In keeping with du Pont's intention to "place in rooms objects most suited to the time and place of the architecture," the Tappahannock Room contains an intriguing

Washington's China

Concerned with keeping collections intact, du Pont set up small display areas in hallways and on stair landings to showcase entire collections, such as the set of porcelain acquired from China and purchased by George Washington (below). The china features the insignia of the Order of the Cincinnati, a hereditary organization founded by Washington and his fellow officers after the Revolution. This technique of massing large numbers of like objects together for maximum visual effect was one that du Pont used many times.

Tree of Life

Made in 1754 by Mary King of Philadelphia, this needlework picture represents a tree of life. The brilliant colors and strong contrasts set it apart from other examples of the same period. King's creativity is evident in the variety of fancy stitches and sophisticated shading.

28

mixture of objects from the Mid-Atlantic region, including architecture from Virginia, furniture from New York and New Jersey, and needlework from Pennsylvania. Once again, the design elements associated with du Pont are plain in an early view of the room: the colors of the Ushak carpet are echoed in a portrait showing a carpet on the table and picked up again in the multicolored earthenware vases atop a New York high chest. Du Pont's love of personal and historical associations can be seen in the objects displayed throughout the room: in the high chest signed by Samuel Clements, a cabinet-maker from Flushing, New York; in the placement of an early clock with works by David Rittenhouse of Philadelphia; and in a

sophisticated silk needlework picture made by Mary King of Philadelphia.

Two of the more remarkable spaces at Winterthur were also installed at this time. In something of a turnabout, du Pont used exterior architecture to create outdoor scenes within his home as a means of displaying outdoor furniture and architectural features. Both the Court and Shop Lane use the facades of historic houses and stores to evoke a bygone era. Du Pont, who preferred to let his collection speak for him, has left no record of his reasons for bringing the out-doors inside.

The Court, placed in the space vacated by the removal of the Badminton Court, is formed by the facades of buildings framing a cobblestone courtyard. This re-creation of an early nineteenth-century village square at dusk is furnished with a remarkable selection of Windsor chairs, representing the many variations of this popular seating form. In addition, the Court displays a collapsible table (believed to have been used by itinerant peddlers) furnished with a wide variety of treen, or wooden, wares. The building exteriors came from three separate areas along the eastern seacoast, and one doorway came from the Connecticut River valley. The facade of Montmorenci, the North Carolina plantation whose interior woodwork is installed elsewhere at Winterthur, dominates the Court.

To the left of Montmorenci stands the rusticated front of a house built in 1750 by a wealthy Newport, Rhode Island,

The Court

The lighting in the Court is dramatic, evoking an early evening scene; the candles are just being lit in the windows of the Red Lion Inn, and twilight is fast fading.

merchant named John Banister. Rustication, a technique also employed at Mount Vernon, features wood that has been cut and painted to look like stone. The Banister house facade faces the brick-front Red Lion Inn, an early 1800s building from Red Lion, Delaware. Two small rooms from the inn have been left in place, allowing visitors to enter the building to view collections of transfer-printed ceramics in the Blue Staffordshire Room and an array of games and gaming devices in the Red Lion Room. At one end of the Red Lion Room, a narrow staircase invites visitors to climb to the second floor of the inn, further enhancing the feeling of having moved from the outside into another world.

Two stories above the Court, du Pont transformed the former bowling alley into an early nineteenth-century shop lane by installing storefronts from New York City; Baltimore, Maryland; and Kingston, New York. Cobblestones pave the narrow street, and iron shop signs lend an air of reality to the scene. Doorways at either end of the lane invite people into the shops—into a New York general store at one end and a shop of Chinese goods at the other.

Shop Lane

Store windows provide a perfect display area for du Pont's large collection of English ceramics, including salt-glazed stonewares and transfer-printed wares. Another window is filled with Chinese export porcelain and one more contains nineteenth-century silver.

32

The Henry Francis du Pont Winterthur Museum

*A*t the beginning of 1951, du Pont formalized his intent to convert Winterthur into a museum. He moved with his family to a new Regency-style home designed by Thomas Waterman. This new home stood opposite the large house that, in October 1951, officially became the Henry Francis du Pont Winterthur Museum. The building Waterman designed, which now houses the Museum Store on Clenny Run, represents the architect's last commission for du Pont; he died in 1951 at age fifty-one. The opening of Winterthur to the public on a regular basis did not mean that du Pont allowed the period room installations to became static. Rather, he turned to a new generation of museum professionals to continue the work of adding to and refining the period rooms that he and Waterman had worked on together.

In the time that had elapsed since du Pont first began his great enterprise of converting his family's house into "an American home," there had been significant advances in the study of American decorative arts. Du Pont and others of his generation had done their work well, inspiring younger collectors and dealers to learn as much as they could about the objects they loved. This new emphasis on scholarship and connoisseurship greatly influenced du Pont. He continued to search out examples of rare and endangered architecture for installation at

Left: Winterthur Museum.

34

What is the colonial revival style?

The term *colonial revival* refers to an approach to interior decoration that gained popularity in the early 1900s. Eager to create and define an identity as an antidote to the seemingly uncontrollable forces of the industrial revolution, Americans turned to the arts and crafts of the eighteenth and early nineteenth centuries, which they felt exemplified the best of the American past. Thus, anything "colonial" became associated with superior craftsmanship, moral integrity, and patriotism.

Winterthur. He did not hesitate to replace a room when better architecture came along or to move paneling from one location to another if space considerations mandated the move. In addition, shortly after Winterthur became a museum, du Pont established a graduate program in American material culture in conjunction with the University of Delaware. Through the Winterthur Program in Early American Culture, research into the decorative arts would be ongoing and conducted in a professional manner.

In the late 1950s, Winterthur staff members visited an abandoned farmhouse, known as the Hehn-Kershner house, in Berks County, Pennsylvania. Built of stone, the house and its outbuildings were excellent architectural examples of the Germanic culture that had taken root in Pennsylvania in the eighteenth century and still flourishes today. Recognizing the significance of the architecture, the museum's professional staff proposed using two rooms from the house (a parlor and the kitchen), several exterior walls, and one outbuilding. They chose to install their new finds in a former basement space that, since 1932, had been the Pine Kitchen.

In many ways, the differences between the Pine Kitchen and the newly acquired Kershner rooms can be seen as direct evidence of the long road traveled by du Pont in his evolution from collector to scholar. The Pine Kitchen (shown at left) was a quintessential colonial revival room. The warm pine paneling, the massing of objects in an attempt to create a homey atmosphere, and the use of hooked rugs all evoke the spirit of a romanticized past. Yet, they do not reflect the reality of a colonial kitchen, which would have had plaster walls that were whitewashed every year to remove the inevitable grease and grime generated by cooking over an open hearth. Only a few kitchen utensils would have been found near the hearth; no rugs would have adorned the floors; and no upholstered easy chairs would have been found in a kitchen, let alone near a fireplace.

In the Kershner Parlor, on the other hand, a great deal of attention and no little trouble centered on keeping the room's original proportions in order to give visitors an impression of the actual relationship of the rooms to one another. In this way it was hoped that the installation created the illusion of the building itself, as was attempted in the Court and Shop Lane. Particular attention was paid to reinstalling an elaborate plasterwork ceiling that had been painstakingly removed, piece by piece, from the original site. In many respects, the plaster ceiling is the centerpiece of the installation, representing an unexpected level of craftsmanship

Kershner Parlor

No form was more desired by Pennsylvania Germans than the tall clock, and inventories reveal that a clock was usually the most expensive piece of furniture in the house.

The ceiling in the original Kershner house being prepared for transport to Winterthur. See the final installation in the Kershner Parlor (above).

from a former frontier region of Pennsylvania.

The furnishing plans for the room commanded the attention of Winterthur's professional staff. They devoted considerable time to researching the family that originally owned the property in order to re-create as faithfully as possible the lifestyle and social customs of the period. Fortunately, Winterthur's collection of Pennsylvania German artifacts was equal to the task. The furnishings included a large wardrobe filled with homespun textiles, a kitchen dresser, a trestle table, a series of plank-seat chairs, a tall-case clock, painted chests, and the slip-decorated earthenware so closely associated with this culture.

Despite this profusion of objects, the room seemed incomplete. In the early 1980s, a group of museum scholars traveled to Germany to conduct research for an upcoming Pennsylvania German exhibition. What they learned caused them to rethink the furnish-

ings of the parlor. The trestle table was moved to the side of the room, and a large bed was installed; this repositioning rein-forced the multiple uses of rooms in the eighteenth century and highlighted the early American custom of placing the "best bed" in a parlor to showcase the expensive textiles that would have adorned it. The plank-seat chairs were replaced by more authentic slat-back chairs. The wardrobe and the tall-case clock, as well as painted chests, continued in residence in the room. This type of rethink-ing and refining of period room displays continues today.

Henry Francis du Pont died in 1969 at the age of eighty-nine. His legacy of con-tinual growth and change, however, remains and continues to influence Winterthur today. Shortly before his death, the Board of Trustees of Winterthur Museum fulfilled one of du Pont's wishes—to have architecture

Georgia Dining Room

Except for lowering the ceiling one foot, this room is installed at Winterthur exactly as it was in the original house, including the placement of the windows and doors.

What is the empire style?

Like the federal style, the empire style relies on classical precedents but with greater historical accuracy. Empire furniture is massive, sculptural, and often highly decorated, such as the Empire Bedroom's dramatic bedroom suite (above) with its architectural-looking columns and cornices enhanced with gilt stenciling and green paint.

from all thirteen of the original colonies represented in Winterthur's collection—by purchasing architecture from Georgia, the only unrepresented colony. Georgia Dining Room, made up of architecture from an 1839 home in Milledgeville, Georgia, replaced the du Pont family's original kitchen area, thus removing the last vestige of a home from the museum. Although du Pont knew of the purchase before his death, the installation was designed and completed afterward, making the Georgia Dining Room the first period room at Winterthur that he did not oversee. Nonetheless, the lessons he taught so well over the years had clearly been learned. The room features wallpaper reproduced from a small fragment found on the original walls when they were brought to Winterthur. The furniture is from the Mid-Atlantic region in the empire style; few pieces of southern furniture survive from the pre–Civil War period, and inventories from the time indicate that wealthy Georgians did, indeed, purchase furniture and furnishings from more urban centers, such as Philadelphia and Baltimore. The draperies are based on a design source from the period, and the room features American-made glassware from one of the nation's newly emerging glassworks.

No collection is ever finished, and Winterthur continues to evolve and grow. Although no new architectural interiors have been added since the Georgia Dining Room, there have been several major changes in the furnishings of the rooms, and the collection range has been expanded to include objects dating as late as 1860. In the early 1990s, Winterthur acquired a significant suite of empire bedroom furniture made by Isaac Jones and owned by the Van Syckel family. The imposing suite, complete with bed, twin wardrobes, dresser, stepping stool, and washstand required a large room with high ceilings. An appropriate space was located in the Franklin Room, a space dedicated to memorabilia honoring Benjamin Franklin. This change necessitated moving the Franklin Room objects to another period room. In another move that reflects the attention to detail established by du Pont, the museum recently acquired a large portrait of the Van Syckel family. The family's portrait is now reunited with the furniture and hangs over the mantel in the renamed Empire Bedroom.

40

The period rooms at Winterthur today represent the many stages of the institution's life. There are rooms that remain much the same as when they were originally designed by Henry Francis du Pont. Some rooms retain his original design intent but with a changing display of objects. Many objects, once displayed in the period rooms, are now on view in the Galleries, a large addition completed in 1992. Ongoing research has shown some objects to be reproductions or to have been altered in some way, and they have been consigned to the study collection, a collection used by students studying American decorative arts. Some rooms have been completely redesigned while others reflect totally new installations. If du Pont were to return to Winterthur today, he undoubtedly would be surprised both by the extent of change and by the extent to which things have remained the same in the period rooms—surprised but not displeased. After spending more than thirty years installing, re-installing, changing, refining, and expanding his period room settings as well as creating the Winterthur Program in Early American Culture, du Pont left clear instructions for his successors. He also left an enduring legacy. Thanks to his foresight, dedication, and discerning eye, the early American arts and crafts have, indeed, been given the recognition they deserve.

Right: Chinese Parlor.

42

Blackwell Parlor.

1926	Henry Francis du Pont inherits Winterthur upon his father's death.
1929–31	First Phase of Period Room Installations at Winterthur: Du Pont remodels and expands the Winterthur house, adding a massive wing that doubles in size the existing building. The first period rooms include: Port Royal Parlor, Readbourne Parlor, Cecil Bedroom, Du Pont Dining Room, Pine Kitchen, and Chinese Parlor.
1933–34	Second Phase of Period Room Installations at Winterthur: Du Pont focuses on historical accuracy and documentation for his period room installations.
	He purchases woodwork from a 1744 home in Lower Marlboro, Maryland, and installs it in the Marlboro Room.
1936	Du Pont replaces the 1902 marble staircase in the original entryway with a spiral staircase from Montmorenci, a North Carolina house built about 1822.
1937–39	Du Pont acquires woodwork from the Stamper-Blackwell house (built about 1764) on Pine Street in Philadelphia and installs it in Blackwell Parlor.
1938	A bedroom from the 1670 Thomas Hart house is installed in the former squash court, which du Pont renames the Hart Room.
	With the help of Bertha Benkard, du Pont installs the Flock Room using woodwork from a 1715 Virginia home.
1947–48	Tappahannock Room, Shop Lane, and the Court are installed.
1951	Winterthur Museum opens to the public, and the Winterthur Program in Early American Culture is established.
	Thomas Waterman, du Pont's chief architect since 1933, dies.
1957–58	The Kershner rooms replace the Pine Kitchen.
1961–67	Air conditioning and humidity control are installed in the museum building.
1969	The death of Henry Francis du Pont marks the end of an era.
1969–72	Georgia Dining Room is installed, thus fulfilling du Pont's wish to have a room from each of the thirteen original colonies at Winterthur.
1989–91	Empire Bedroom is installed.
1992	The Galleries at Winterthur, a 22,000-square-foot display area, opens to the public.

43

To learn more about Henry Francis du Pont's development of the Winterthur
property, see *Discover the Winterthur Estate* by Pauline K. Eversmann with
Kathryn H. Head.